The N Cheesecake Cookbook

Give Your Oven a Rest with

These Simple

Cheesecake Recipes

Table of Contents

Introduction 4
1. Unbaked cherry cheesecake 6
2. No bake sugar free cheesecake 8
3. 3 step cheesecake 11
4. No-bake lemon cheesecake 14
5. Mini raspberry cheesecakes 17
6. Strawberry cheesecake in a jar 20
7. No bake lime cheesecake 23
8. Amaretto Mousse cheesecakes 26
9. No bake apple cheesecake 29
10. Amaretto cheesecake II 31
11. Easy no-bake cheesecake 34
12. Chocolate No-bake cheesecake 37
13. Avocado Cheesecake 39
14. Raspberry swirl 42
15. No-bake Peach cheesecake 45
16. Mixed Berry cheesecake 47
17. Pumpkin Pie Cheesecake 49
18. Green Tea cheesecake 51
19. Oreo No-Bake cheesecake 54
20. Nutella No-Bake cheesecake 57
21. No-Bake cherry cheesecake 59
22. Light and Fluffy No-Bake cheesecake 61
23. Mini blueberry cheesecake 63
24. Chocolate Turtles Cheesecake 66
25. Lemon cherry no-bake cheesecake 69
26. Mocha no-bake cheesecake 72
27. Ricotta chocolate cheesecake 74
28. Pumpkin pie no-bake cheesecake 77
29. No-bake strawberry cheesecake 80

30. Peanut butter Cheesecake 83

Conclusion 86

Introduction

I am not embarrassed to admit that I have a passion for cheesecake bordering on addiction. From dense and creamy graham cracker crusted vanilla to light and fluffy frozen cheesecake bars, I love them all! If you feel the same way, the read on my kindred spirit and find that perfect combination of ingredients to make your ideal dessert.

You may be worried that cheesecake could be too dense and fill if you have just served your guests an exquisite steak with mashed potatoes and gravy. I understand your misgivings but am here to say that even the most filling of meals can benefit from a light cake that is moist and delicious you

I just want to add a note that no-bake means the filling does not need baking in an oven before serving. There are some entries here that do require the crust to be baked to become firm, although you could probably do this just as efficiently in the refrigerator. If you do by-pass the oven altogether, then double the time required for the crust to set.

1. Unbaked cherry cheesecake

Pair this cheesecake with a lovely late-season Riesling to bring out the sweet taste of the berries. Belgian cherry beer also complements this scrumptious dessert and makes for a unique drink to serve your guests.

Preparation Time-30 minutes

Servings –12

Ingredients

- 10 ounces graham cracker crumbs
- 2 ounces softened margarine
- 2 ounces sugar

- 8 ounces cream cheese
- 8 ounces powdered sugar
- 1 teaspoon vanilla extract
- 8 ounces whipped heavy cream
- 12 ½ ounces cherry pie filling

Directions

1. Mix crumbs, margarine and sugar in a large bowl until well combined

2. In a 10" pie plate, press the mixture evenly all the way around and up the sides

3. In another bowl, beat the cream cheese, vanilla and sugar until it forms a smooth spread

4. Pour the cheese into the crust and even it out with a wooden spoon

5. Chill for 3 hours, remove and spread the cherry filling over the top evenly

6. Refrigerator for another 30 minutes and serve

2. No bake sugar free cheesecake

If you are making a sugar-free cake, then chances are you don't want to serve a high-fructose beverage to accompany it. This cheesecake matches well with a strong coffee flavored with some caramel or vanilla.

Preparation Time-15 minutes

Servings –9

Ingredients

- 14 ounces graham cracker crumbs
- 4 ounces butter

- 1/2 teaspoon cinnamon, ground
- 6 ounces lemon flavored Jello
- 8 ounces boiling water
- 8 ounces softened cream cheese
- 1/3 ounce vanilla extract
- 8 ounces thawed frozen whipped topping,

Directions

1. Preheat the oven to 350 degrees Fahrenheit

2. Combine butter, 13 ounces of crumbs, and cinnamon in a large bowl and mix well

3. Press the crumb mixture to form a crust in the bottom of the pie plate

4. Bake for about 10 minutes, remove and set aside

5. Pour gelatin in the boiling water and stir until completely dissolved. Let the mixture thicken without allowing it to set

6. Beat the cheese and vanilla in a large bowl until smooth and then add the gelatin to the cheese, blending well

7. Fold in the whipped topping to the mixture in the bowl

8. Transfer the filling into the pie crust and use a spatula to even it out

9. Sprinkle crumbs over top and chill overnight

3. 3 step cheesecake

This dish is a straightforward vanilla cheesecake recipe that is like a blank canvas to create any dessert masterpiece you desire. I like to keep it simple by adding some fresh fruit and a white chocolate curl, but you can also add whipped topping or sweet sauce.

Preparation Time-10 minutes

Servings –8

Ingredients

- 1 full package of graham crackers
- 5 ½ ounces of melted unsalted butter
- 1 ounce sugar
- 16 ounces softened cream cheese
- 10 ounces condensed milk, sweetened
- 2 ounces fresh lemon juice

Directions

2. Put graham crackers in a blender or food processor and grind into a fine crumb consistency

3. Combine crumbs, sugar and butter in a large bowl and mix well

4. Create a crust in a 9" springform pan by pressing the crumbs down along the bottom

5. Chill the crust for 30 minutes

6. Beat cream cheese in a bowl with an electric mixer until smooth

7. Add milk and beat until combined, then lemon juice and vanilla

8. Pour filling into the pan over the crust, cover and chill for 3 hours

9. Remove the springform ring from cheesecake and serve

4. No-bake lemon cheesecake

Lemon cheesecake is difficult to pair because the sour taste of the lemon usually overpowers the flavor of any wine that you might try. Try a shot of limoncello in some ice wine if the lemon flavor is intense.

Preparation Time-30 minutes

Servings –24

Ingredients

- 9" pie plate
- 24 ounces graham cracker crumbs
- 4 ounces butter
- ½ ounce confectioners' sugar
- 3 ounces lemon flavored jello
- 8 ounces boiling water
- 8 ounces softened cream cheese
- 8 ounces white sugar
- 1 teaspoon vanilla extract
- 5 ounces evaporated milk

Directions

1. Preheat oven to 350 degrees Fahrenheit

2. Combine crumbs, butter and sugar in a large bowl and mix well

3. Press the crumbs in the bottom of the pie plate to form a crust.

4. Bake crust for 10 minutes, remove from heat and set aside to cool

5. Stir the gelatin in a glass with boiling water and let it dissolve completely

6. Set the gelatin aside and let it thicken but don't let it set

7. Beat cream cheese, sugar and vanilla in a bowl until smooth and set aside

8. Whip evaporated milk in a separate bowl until you see peaks forming

9. Add gelatin and mix in with the evaporated milk, then fold cream cheese in slowly

10. Pour the filling into the pie plate and refrigerate for 4 hours

5. Mini raspberry cheesecakes

The trick to pairing wine with sweet desserts is the delicate balance between the sweetness of the grape and the overall sugar in the cheesecake. With these raspberry treats, I would stick with a dry white wine otherwise the puree might overpower the drink.

Preparation Time-15 minutes

Servings –12

Ingredients

- 6 ounces graham cracker crumbs
- 2 ounces pecans, chopped
- 1 ½ ounces melted butter
- 6 ounces crushed fresh raspberries
- 4 ounces softened cream cheese
- 10 ½ ounces condensed milk, sweetened
- 8 ounces thawed frozen whipped topping

Directions

1. Line a muffin tin with paper liners (12 cups)

2. Combine crumbs, pecans and margarine in a bowl and blend well

3. Spoon even amounts of the crust into the bottom of the muffin tins and press down with a spoon or a cork to even out

4. Put raspberries into a food processor and puree. Set them aside

5. In a separate bowl, beat cream cheese until smooth, then add milk and half of the fruit puree. Mix well and fold in whipped topping

6. Separate the puree mixture evenly in the muffin cups and put the tin in the freezer for 6 hours

7. Garnish the top with the rest of the puree and some whole fruit if desired and serve

6. Strawberry cheesecake in a jar

Strawberries provide a more tart taste than other berries because of the small amount of sugar they contain. I like to spread fresh fruits throughout the jar to cut the sweetness of the cheese filling, and this also creates a nice layering effect.

Preparation Time-20 minutes

Servings –4

Ingredients

- 12 ounces graham cracker crumbs
- 4 ounces melted butter
- 2 ounce white sugar
- 4 canning jars, half pints
- 8 ounces softened cream cheese
- 8 ounces thawed frozen whipped topping
- 5 ½ ounces white sugar
- 1 teaspoon vanilla extract
- 4 sliced strawberries

Directions

1. Add crumbs, butter and 2 ounces of sugar in a bowl and mix well

2. Separate the crumb mixture evenly in each jar and press down to flatten the crumbs

3. Beat cream cheese and whipped topping in a large bowl until completely combined

4. Beat 5 ½ ounces of sugar and vanilla into the cream cheese until you see peaks forming

5. Separate the mixture from the bowl into the jars and garnish with strawberries

6. Chill for 1 hour before serving

7. No bake lime cheesecake

If you are serving this at a summer party, then why not mix up some Margaritas to complement the subtle sour taste of the lime. These delicious drinks are not too tart, so they will bring out the flavor of the cheesecake while not overpowering it.

Preparation Time-45 minutes

Servings –12

Ingredients

- 16 ounces gingersnap cookie crumbs
- 1 ounce white sugar
- 2 ½ ounces butter, melted
- ¼ ounce unflavored gelatin
- 5 ½ ounce lime juice
- 12 ounces heavy cream, divided
- 9 ounces chopped white chocolate
- 24 ounces softened cream cheese
- 8 ounces white sugar
- 1 ounce lime zest, grated

Directions

1. Combine crumbs, sugar and butter in a large bowl and mix well

2. Form a crust in the bottom of a 10" cake pan by pressing the crumbs down evenly

3. Add lime juice and gelatin together in a separate bowl and set aside

4. Put chocolate in another bowl

5. Simmer 4 ounces of whipping cream in a saucepan, remove from heat, and pour over the chocolate

6. Allow chocolate and whipping cream to melt and soften until smooth.

7. Add the gelatin and lime mixture to the chocolate and mix gently

8. Let it cool to room temperature

9. Add 16 ounces of cream to the chocolate and beat until you see peaks forming

10. Beat cream cheese and sugar in a bowl until mixed thoroughly

11. Slowly add chocolate to the cream cheese, then lime zest

12. Fold the whipped cream into the mixture and transfer to the cake pan

13. Cover with wrap and chill overnight

8. Amaretto Mousse cheesecakes

Peach is often a flavor that is paired with amaretto because the nutty taste of the liqueur tastes divine with the subtle sweetness of this juicy fruit. Try a peach flavored wine with this cheesecake and your taste buds will thank you.

Preparation Time-15 minutes

Servings –12

Ingredients

- 16 ounces graham cracker crumbs
- 4 ounces melted butter
- ¼ ounce unflavored gelatin
- 4 ounces cold water
- 24 ounces softened cream cheese
- 10 ounces white sugar
- 5 ounces evaporated milk
- 1 teaspoon vanilla extract
- 1 teaspoon lemon juice
- 2 ½ ounces amaretto liqueur
- 6 ounces heavy cream

Directions

1. Combine crumbs and butter in a bowl and mix thoroughly

2. Create a crust in a 9" baking pan by pressing the crumbs down evenly in the bottom

3. Put the baking pan in the refrigerator for a few minutes to cool

4. Dissolve gelatin in water and set aside

5. Beat cream cheese and sugar in a bowl until smooth

6. Slowly add milk, vanilla and lemon juice, stirring gently

7. Scrape the bowl to ensure there is no lumpy residue

8. Add gelatin and liqueur and combine well

9. Whip cream in a separate bowl until you see peaks forming, then fold into the cream cheese

10. Spread the filling over the crust and chill overnight

9. No bake apple cheesecake

With the cold weather outside, a hard apple cider tastes beautiful when served with this simple cheesecake. The cider will warm the belly and will cut some of the sweetness of the dessert.

Preparation Time-30 minutes

Servings –12

Ingredients

- 16 ounces softened cream cheese
- 16 ounces thawed frozen whipped topping
- 8 ounces white sugar
- 1 teaspoon vanilla extract
- 21 ounces of canned apple pie filling
- 9" graham cracker crust

Directions

1. Beat vanilla, sugar and cream cheese in a bowl until smooth. Fold in whipped cream

2. Pour the filling into the crust, pour the apple pie filling over top and chill for 2 hours

10. Amaretto cheesecake II

One word describes the best kind of wine to serve with this cheesecake, and that word is dry. To cut the sweetness of the liqueur choose a Sauvignon-Blanc or Malbec to complement the unique taste of this cheesecake.

Preparation Time-5 minutes

Servings –12

Ingredients

- 16 ounces graham cracker crumbs
- 4 ounces melted butter
- ¼ ounce unflavored gelatin
- 4 ounces water
- 24 ounces softened cream cheese
- 10 ounces white sugar
- 5 ounces evaporated milk
- 1 teaspoon lemon juice
- 2 ½ ounces amaretto liqueur
- 1 teaspoon vanilla extract
- 6 ounces heavy whipping cream

Directions

1. Stir crumbs and melted butter together until well combined

2. Create a crust by putting and pressing the crumbs into the bottom of a 9" spring-form pan

3. Chill for 30 minutes or until firm

4. Add cold water and gelatin to a saucepan. Set aside for 60 seconds

5. Put saucepan on Low heat and cook until gelatin is dissolved completely. Remove from heat and let cool

6. Beat cream cheese and sugar together in a bowl until smooth

7. Slowly beat amaretto liqueur into the mixture, then vanilla and then the gelatin until well combined.

8. Whip cream in a separate bowl until you see stiff peaks forming, then fold into the liqueur mixture

9. Pour filling over the crust in the pan and chill 12-24 hours

10. When you feel confident that the cake has set, remove spring-form ring

11. Easy no-bake cheesecake

The lemon and cherry in this dessert reduce the amount of sweet and sour, so you don't need to worry about the beverage you are pairing it with overpowering the cake. I prefer a lovely Riesling with this recipe because it is still dry enough that you can taste the sweetness of the cheese.

Preparation Time-30 minutes

Servings –12

Ingredients

- 12 ounces graham cracker crumbs
- 2 ½ ounces brown sugar, packed
- 1/2 teaspoon cinnamon, ground
- 2 ½ ounces melted butter
- 16 ounces softened cream cheese
- 1/3 ounce lemon juice
- 16 ounces heavy whipping cream
- 2 ½ ounces white sugar
- 21 ounces canned cherry pie filling

Directions

1. Stir crumbs, brown sugar, cinnamon and butter into a small bowl and mix well

2. Create a crust in a 10" spring-form cake pan by pressing the crumbs down evenly on the bottom. Chill in the refrigerator for 30 minutes or until firm

3. Beat cream cheese and lemon juice together in a separate bowl with an electric mixer until thick and smooth

4. Slowly add sugar and beat until you see stiff peaks forming

5. Pour filling into the pie crust and chill for another 30 minutes.

6. Remove the pan from the cheesecake once set and serve

12. Chocolate No-bake cheesecake

Sweet red wine is the best pairing for this simple and delicious cheesecake. I would recommend Brachetto d'Acqui DOCG or a Zinfandel to accompany your dessert.

Preparation Time-15 minutes

Servings –10

Ingredients

- 2 squares semi-sweet chocolate
- 16 ounces softened cream cheese

- 2 ½ ounces sugar
- 16 ounces chocolate dip made by Cool Whip
- 6 ounce pie crust, Oreo
- 12 ounces strawberries, cut in half

Directions

1. Put chocolate in a microwave-safe bowl and cook on high for 60 seconds or until melted completely.

2. With an electric mixer, beat cream cheese and sugar together until you see stiff peaks form and the consistency is smooth

3. Add chocolate to the cream cheese, mix thoroughly, then slowly add chocolate dip

4. Pour over the Oreo crust and chill for 3-4 hours

5. Garnish with strawberries and serve

13. Avocado Cheesecake

The creamy avocado combined with the lemon zest makes this no-too sweet cheesecake a perfect match with a sweet wine like a Riesling or Moscato. I like to serve this with some crushed walnuts on the side for sprinkling just before serving to add an extra nutty flavor.

Preparation Time-15 minutes

Servings –10

Ingredients

- 6 ounces walnuts, shelled
- 8 ounces graham cracker crumbs
- ½ ounce sugar
- 1/2 teaspoon anise seeds, crushed
- 1/4 teaspoon salt
- ¼ ounce unflavored gelatin
- Zest from 1 lemon
- 12 ounces skim milk
- 4 ounce sugar
- 1 teaspoon vanilla extract
- 2 ripened and pitted avocados, peeled and diced
- 8 ounces softened cream cheese, cut in small pieces

Directions

1. Heat oven to 350 degrees Fahrenheit

2. Put walnuts into a food processor and grind finely on pulse

3. Add crumbs, ½ ounce sugar, seeds and salt and pulse until well combined

4. Add 1 ounce of water and blend until the mixture looks sandy and wet

5. Form a crust with the crumbs along the bottom of an 9" spring-from pan by pressing down evenly

6. Bake for 20 minutes, remove from heat and let cool

7. Dissolve gelatin in 1 ounce of water and set aside for 5 minutes

8. Combine milk, 4 ounces of sugar and lemon zest and bring to a boil

9. Add gelatin and simmer for 1 minute or until gelatin has dissolved

10. Strain the mixture and remove zest

11. Combine avocados and cream cheese in a blender, then add milk. Blend until smooth

12. Spread the mixture into the crust and chill for 2-3 hours or until set

13. Remove spring-form ring and serve

14. Raspberry swirl

The swirly raspberry is visually appealing in this delicious and fluffy cheesecake. Berries usually pair well with a medium-dry white wine like Riesling to complement the sweetness of the fruit rather than overpower it.

Preparation Time-60 minutes

Servings –24

Ingredients

- 24 ounces graham cracker crumbs
- 1 1/4 teaspoons cinnamon, ground
- 16 ounces white sugar
- 4 ounces melted butter
- 4 egg yolks
- 8 ounces softened cream cheese
- 4 egg whites
- 1/4 teaspoon cream of tartar
- 1/8 teaspoon salt
- 2 ounces white sugar
- 8 ounces thawed frozen whipped topping
- 10 ounces thawed frozen raspberries

Directions

1. Preheat oven to 350 degrees Fahrenheit

2. Combine crumbs, cinnamon, sugar and butter in a large bowl and mix thoroughly

3. Create a crust in the bottom of a rectangular baking pan (9"x13") and press down to even it out

4. Put in the oven for 5 minutes to firm up, remove from heat and set aside to cool

5. Beat egg yolks in a separate bowl for 5 minutes or until thick and yellow In Add cream cheese to the egg yolks and beat until smooth, gradually increasing the speed

6. Beat egg whites, tartar and salt in a separate bowl until frothy

7. Add 2 ounces of sugar gradually, beating into the egg white mixture until you see peaks forming

8. Fold one third of the egg white mixture into the cheese, then reverse the process and fold the cheese into the rest of the egg whites

9. Add the whipped topping by folding it into the cheese mixture

10. Put raspberries in a food processor and puree

11. Layer cheese and puree in the baking dish by adding first the cheese, then puree, then cheese, then finishing with the rest of the raspberries

12. Freeze for 30 minutes or until firm

15. No-bake Peach cheesecake

This peach cheesecake recipe pairs well with citrus ale or brandy to complement the fruity flavor. I love serving this dish with some juicy peach slices decoratively placed on top of each serving.

Preparation Time-15 minutes

Servings –16

Ingredients

- 16 ounces softened cream cheese
- 4 ounces confectioners' sugar
- 1 teaspoon vanilla extract
- 24 ounces peach preserves
- 8 ounces whipped topping
- 2 x 8" prepared graham cracker crusts

Directions

1. In a large mixing bowl, beat cream cheese with an electric mixer until you see soft peaks forming

2. Gradually add sugar to the cream cheese and continue to beat until well combined

3. Add vanilla and peach preserves and mix all Ingredients well

4. Add whipped cream to the cream cheese mixture by gently folding until smooth and even

5. Separate filling between the two crusts and chill for 1-2 hours

16. Mixed Berry cheesecake

The mixed berries in this cheesecake create a refreshing flavor that is not too sweet and not too tart. A dry white wine with similar features like a Sauvignon Blanc pairs well with this delectable dessert.

Preparation Time-15 minutes

Servings –16

Ingredients

- 10 ounces graham cracker crumbs
- 2 ounces melted butter,
- 17 ½ ounces softened Cream Cheese
- 6 ounces sugar

- 32 ounces mixed fresh berries
- 16 ounces thawed frozen whipped topping

Directions

1. Combine crumbs and butter in a bowl

2. Create crust in a 9" pie pan by pressing the crumbs down along the bottom

3. Chill the crust for 20 minutes

4. Beat cream cheese and sugar with an electric mixer in a large bowl until well combined

5. In a small dish, press a fork or bottom of a spoon into 12 ounces of berries, mashing them

6. Mix the berries in with the cream cheese and beat on low speed for 5 minutes or until lightly blended

7. Gradually stir in whipped topping and pour the filling over the crust

8. Chill for 6-8 hours

9. Garnish with the rest of the berries before serving

17. Pumpkin Pie Cheesecake

Pumpkin is a traditional fall treat that I use in many desserts and puddings around my house. I like to decorate this pumpkin cheesecake with some shaved chocolate and pecans for a festive holiday look.

Preparation Time-20 minutes

Servings –8

Ingredients

- 8 ounces softened package cream cheese
- ½ ounce milk
- ½ ounce white sugar

- 8 ounces thawed whipped topping, divided
- 6 ounces graham cracker crust
- 15 ounces canned pumpkin puree
- 8 ounces milk
- 7 ounces instant vanilla pudding mix
- 1 teaspoon cinnamon, ground
- 1/2 teaspoon ginger, ground
- 1/4 teaspoon cloves, ground

Directions

1. Combine cream cheese, ½ ounce of milk and sugar in a bowl and beat with an electric mixer until well blended

2. Add half of the whipped topping and stir thoroughly

3. Pour the filling into the crust and spread evenly

4. In another bowl, add pumpkin, 8 ounces of milk, pudding, cinnamon, ginger and cloves and whisk until blended and of a thick consistency

5. Spread the pumpkin mix over the cream cheese and chill for 4 hours

6. Cover with the rest of the whipped topping and serve

18. Green Tea cheesecake

Green tea is a unique flavor for cheesecake that is not too sweet and creates a lovely tinge in the color of the cheese. If I want to get creative, I will add a little bit of green food coloring to the filling to emphasize the included Ingredients.

Preparation Time-20 minutes

Servings –6

Ingredients

- 9 ounces graham cracker crumbs, finely crushed
- 1 ¾ ounces melted unsalted butter
- 7 ounces softened cream cheese
- 3 ounces white sugar

- 1 teaspoon white sugar
- 7 ounces mascarpone cheese
- 2 ounces green tea powder, divided
- 8 ounces heavy whipping cream
- ½ ounce unflavored gelatin
- 1 ½ ounces warm water
- 1 teaspoon confectioners' sugar
- 3 sliced strawberries

Directions

1. Mix crumbs and butter in a bowl and create a crust with the mixture by pressing it down in the bottom of a 7" springform pan. Chill for 20 minutes

2. In a large bowl, beat 3 ounces + 1 teaspoon of sugar and all of the cream cheese together until you see peaks forming

3. Add the mascarpone cheese and beat until well combined

4. Stir in 1 ½ ounces of green tea powder into the cream cheese

5. Chill a metal bowl for 20 minutes, then add cream to the bowl and beat until you see peaks forming

6. Fold the whipped cream into the cream cheese

7. In another bowl, dissolve gelatin in water

8. Transfer the cream cheese to the gelatin in the bowl and stir until well combined

9. Spread the filling over the crust and chill for 4 hours

10. Sprinkle with the rest of the green tea powder and sugar

11. Decorate with strawberry slices before serving

19. Oreo No-Bake cheesecake

You don't necessarily need to use the brand Oreo for this recipe, any chocolate sandwich cookie with vanilla filling will work. The chocolate of the cookies in this recipe pairs nicely with a lovely port or Zinfandel.

Preparation Time-20 minutes

Servings –16

Ingredients

- 18 ounces oreo cookies, divided
- 2 ounces melted butter
- 32 ounces softened cream cheese
- 6 ounces sugar
- 1 teaspoon vanilla
- 8 ounces thawed frozen whipped topping

Directions

1. Place 15 cookies on a flat surface and chop coarsely. Set aside

2. Put the rest of the cookies in a food processor and grind. Transfer the ground cookies to a bowl and mix with the butter.

3. Create a crust with the butter and cookie mixture by pressing down into a 9"x13" pan evenly

4. Chill for 30 minutes

5. In a big bowl, beat cream cheese, sugar and vanilla in a bowl with a mixer until well combined

6. Stir whipped topping in gradually to the cream cheese mixture, then add the chopped cookies

7. Spread over the crust evenly and chill for 4 hours

20. Nutella No-Bake cheesecake

You will love the combination of nutty and chocolate flavors in this creamy cheesecake. I like to pair this with a cream sherry when I am looking for unique beverages to serve after dinner.

Preparation Time-10 minutes

Servings –8

Ingredients

- 16 ounces softened cream cheese
- 4 ounces white sugar
- 13 ounces Nutella spread
- 1/4 teaspoon vanilla extract
- 9" graham cracker crust

Directions

1. Beat cream cheese and sugar in a bowl with an electric mixer until you see peaks forming

2. Mix Nutella and vanilla into the cream cheese until well combined

3. Spread the filling in the crust and chill overnight

21. No-Bake cherry cheesecake

When using a sweet topping like fruit filling, it is best to serve the dessert with dry white wine or another drink that doesn't add to the sugary taste. A nice hot cup of coffee will also do the trick when your guests are ready to bite into this delicious cheesecake after their meal.

Preparation Time-15 minutes

Servings –9

Ingredients

- 20 finely crushed graham crackers

- 4 ounces confectioners' sugar
- 2 ounces melted butter
- 8 ounces softened cream cheese
- 8 ounces thawed frozen whipped topping
- 8 ounces confectioners' sugar
- 12 ounces canned cherry pie filling

Directions

1. Add crumbs, 4 ounces of sugar and butter into a bowl and mix well

2. Create a crust by pressing the mixture into the bottom of a 9"x9" pan

3. Chill the crust while you make the filling

4. In a large bowl, whisk cream cheese, frozen topping and 8 ounces of sugar together until smooth

5. Spread the cream cheese over the crust, then top with the cherry pie filling

6. Chill for 2 hours

22. Light and Fluffy No-Bake cheesecake

The name says it all for this airy cheesecake recipe. Even after a heavy meal, this delicious dessert will satisfy that sweet tooth while letting you bask in the satisfaction of a beautiful dinner and still able to move.

Preparation Time-30 minutes

Servings –10

Ingredients

- 8 ounces softened cream cheese
- 2 ½ ounces white sugar
- 8 ounces thawed frozen whipped topping
- 9 " graham cracker crust

Directions

1. Add cream cheese and sugar to a large bowl, and mix together until you see peaks forming

2. Fold the whipped topping into the cream cheese slowly

3. Spread the cream cheese mixture into the crust and chill for 4 hours

23. Mini blueberry cheesecake

When making a cheesecake that has berries for the topping or filling, it is a good idea to buy wine that matches the sweetness of the fruit. For blueberries, Asti Spumante makes one of the best pairings and complements the creamy texture of the cheese as well.

Preparation Time-30 minutes

Servings –15

Ingredients

- 16 ounces graham cracker crumbs
- 4 ounces melted butter
- 8 ounces softened cream cheese
- 2 ounces milk
- 1 ounce confectioners' sugar
- 21 ounces blueberry pie filling
- 8 ounces heavy whipping cream
- 1 ½ ounces white sugar
- 1 teaspoon vanilla extract

Directions

1. Mix crumbs and butter together in a bowl and set aside 4 ounces of this mixture

2. Create a crust with the rest of the crumbs by pressing them into the bottom of a baking pan 7"x11" and chilling for 30 minutes in the refrigerator

3. Beat cream cheese, confectioners' sugar and milk in a bowl with an electric mixer until smooth and you see peaks forming

4. Spread the cream cheese over the crust, then the pie filling over the cream cheese. Chill for another 30 minutes

5. Whip cream, white sugar and vanilla in bowl with a mixer, then spread this whipped cream mixture over the pie filling

6. Sprinkle the rest of the crumbs and butter over the top of the whipped cream and chill for 1 hour

24. Chocolate Turtles Cheesecake

This chocolate cheesecake is decadent and sweet, so it is best for after a light meal of fish or white meat. You can substitute real turtles for the chocolate and caramel found in the **Ingredients**.

Preparation Time-30 minutes

Servings –12

Ingredients

- 9 " Oreo cookie crust
- 7 ounces caramel candy
- 2 ounces evaporated milk

- 6 ounces pecans, chopped
- 6 ounces softened cream cheese
- 4 ounces sour cream
- 10 ounces milk
- 4 ounces instant chocolate pudding mix
- 4 ounces chocolate fudge topping

Directions

1. In a saucepan with a heavy bottom, cook caramels and evaporated milk on medium heat for 5 minutes or until smooth. Stir frequently.

2. Add 4 ounces of pecans to the saucepan and stir

3. Pour the caramel mixture into the crust and set aside

4. Blend cream cheese, sour cream and milk in a food processor until smooth. Add pudding and blend for another 30 seconds

5. Pour the mixture from the food processor over the caramel in the crust and chill for 30 minutes

6. Gently pour the fudge topping over the cake by drizzling in unique shapes

7. Sprinkle the top with the rest of the chopped pecans and chill for another 30 minutes

25. Lemon cherry no-bake cheesecake

As mentioned previously, the combination of the lemon and cherry reduces the amount of tart in the cheesecake and adds a lovely mild sweet taste that is not too intense. Espresso is a beautiful addition to this dessert, but if you want something alcoholic, you can add brandy to strong coffee.

Preparation Time-20 minutes

Servings –24

Ingredients

- 20 ounces graham cracker crumbs
- 4 ounces melted butter
- 6 ounces lemon flavored Jello
- 8 ounces boiling water
- 8 ounces softened cream cheese
- 8 ounces white sugar
- 1 teaspoon vanilla extract
- 1 ½ ounces lemon juice
- 12 fluid ounces evaporated milk
- 21 ounces cherry pie filling

Directions

1. Mix together the crumbs and melted butter

2. Create a crust with the mixture by pressing it into the bottom of a baking pan (9"x13"). Chill for 10 minutes

3. Add gelatin to the boiling water and stir to dissolve. Set aside.

4. Beat cream cheese, sugar and vanilla in a large bowl with an electric mixer until smooth

5. Add gelatin and lemon juice, stirring thoroughly

6. Whip evaporated milk in another bowl until frothy, then fold the milk into the cream cheese.

7. Pour cream cheese into the pan and chill for 5 hours

8. Spread pie filling over the top when you are ready to serve

26. Mocha no-bake cheesecake

Any powdered coffee mixture with mocha and cappuccino flavors included will do for this creamy cake. The chocolate flavor pairs well with some red wine, or you can serve a cappuccino made from the same brew as the Ingredients.

Preparation Time-15 minutes

Servings –8

Ingredients

- 2 ounces Chocolate, Semi-Sweet
- ½ ounce butter
- 1 9" Oreo cookie crust
- 8 ounces softened cream cheese

- 2 ½ ounces sugar
- 2 ½ ounces swiss mocha coffee powder
- 16 ounces thawed frozen whipped topping

Directions

1. In a microwavable bowl, combine chocolate and butter and cook in microwave on high for 60 seconds. Stir mixture until well combined

2. Spread the melted chocolate on the crust and chill for 20 minutes

3. In a large bowl, beat cream cheese and sugar with a mixer until smooth

4. Add the powdered coffee and stir thoroughly

5. Gradually stir in frozen whipped topping

6. Spread the whipped topping mixture over the cream cheese and chill for 4 hours

27. Ricotta chocolate cheesecake

The ricotta cheese cuts the sweetness of the chocolate cookies in this delectable cheesecake recipe. Serve this dessert with some of the same liqueur used in the method or a slightly different nut-flavored version.

Preparation Time-30 minutes

Servings –10

Ingredients

- 12 ounces chocolate cookies, crushed
- 1 ½ ounces butter
- 20 ounces ricotta cheese
- 8 ounces confectioners' sugar
- 1 teaspoon vanilla extract
- 1 ounce candied lemon and orange peel, chopped finely
- 1 ounce creme de cacao liqueur
- 2 ounces of grated bittersweet chocolate
- 4 ounces heavy cream
- ½ ounce confectioners' sugar
- 2 ounces grated bittersweet chocolate

Directions

1. Combine cookies and butter in a bowl and mix together thoroughly

2. Create a crust in the bottom of a 9" springform pan by pressing the crumbs into the bottom evenly

3. Chill for 20 minutes

4. Beat ricotta, 8 ounces of confectioners' sugar and vanilla in a large bowl with a mixer until fluffy

5. Add peel and 2 ounces of chocolate to the ricotta cheese mixture and stir thoroughly

6. Pour the filling into the crust and chill overnight

7. When you are ready to serve, whip cream in a large bowl with a ½ ounce of sugar until you see peaks forming

8. Remove the springform ring from the cake and spread the whipped topping evenly over the top

9. Sprinkle with the rest of the chocolate and serve

28. Pumpkin pie no-bake cheesecake

I have friends who kick up the spice in this recipe by doubling the cinnamon, nutmeg, and ginger and then include pumpkin spice in the whipped cream topping. I have tried the resulting cheesecake, and I find that less is more when it comes to the spice in the Ingredients.

Preparation Time-20 minutes

Servings –8

Ingredients

- 8 ounces package low-fat cream cheese
- 2 ½ ounces white sugar
- 1 1/2 tablespoons lemon juice
- 1 1/2 teaspoons vanilla extract
- 15 ounces canned pumpkin puree
- 1 teaspoon cinnamon, ground
- 1/2 teaspoon ginger, ground
- 1/2 teaspoon nutmeg, ground
- 4 ounces heavy whipping cream
- 9" graham cracker crust

Directions

1. Combine cream cheese and sugar in a bowl and mix well. Add lemon juice and vanilla and stir until combined.

2. Add half of the puree, cinnamon, ginger and nutmeg and fold into the cream cheese

3. Beat cream in a chilled bowl until you see peaks forming and fold whipped cream and the rest of the pumpkin puree into the cream cheese

4. Spread the filling on the crust evenly, cover and chill for 4 hours

29. No-bake strawberry cheesecake

A lovely way to serve this cheesecake is to decorate the top with a fresh mixed-berry medley and some whipped topping. Berries pair well with Zinfandel or late-season Riesling if you want to serve this dessert with something alcoholic.

Preparation Time-20 minutes

Servings –10

Ingredients

- 3 ounces gelatin, strawberry-flavored
- 8 ounces boiling water
- 8 ounces softened cream cheese,
- 8 ounces white sugar
- 1 teaspoon vanilla extract
- 5 ounces canned evaporated milk, chilled
- 9" graham cracker crust

Directions

1. In a glass dish, stir gelatin in boiling water until dissolved, then chill for 20 minutes, making sure it is firm but not set

2. Beat cheese, sugar and vanilla with an electric mixer until smooth

3. Beat milk until thick and the consistency of whipped cream in another bowl

4. Slowly add the gelatin to the milk, beating with the mixer until well combined

5. Fold cream cheese into gelatin until it reaches consistency of thickened filling

6. Pour filling into the crust and chill for 4 hours

30. Peanut butter Cheesecake

The combination of chocolate and peanut butter is a favorite around my house, so I have made this cheesecake more than once to rave reviews. I would serve this cheesecake with a spiced tea or strong coffee to warm the belly and aid in digestion.

Preparation Time-20 minutes

Servings –12

Ingredients

- 10 ounces chocolate sandwich cookie crumbs
- 2 ounces melted butter
- 9 ounces softened cream cheese
- 8 ounces smooth peanut butter
- 8 ounces white sugar
- 7 ounces chopped Toblerone bars, divided
- 12 ounces thawed frozen whipped topping, divided

Directions

1. In a small bowl, mix cookie crumbs and butter until well combined.

2. Form a crust in the bottom of a 9" springform pan and press down until surface is even

3. Chill for 20 minutes

4. Combine cream cheese, smooth peanut butter and sugar with an electric mixer until smooth

5. Stir in half of the chocolate and mix thoroughly

6. Whisk in 8 ounces of frozen whipped topping

7. Pour the mixture over the crust and chill for 4 hours

8. Put the rest of the whipped topping in the microwave and cook on high for 60 seconds. Pour the heated topping over the cheesecake and chill for 1 hour or until firm

9. Remove springform ring before serving

Conclusion

When you are looking for an easy dessert that will wow your guests and complements your meal, then look no further than a no-bake cheesecake. From chocolate to pumpkin to fruity frozen bars, the recipes in this cookbook will give you plenty of options to choose from when trying to decide on the perfect dessert. The pairings mentioned are suggestions from my own experience, but there are hundreds of options of liqueurs, hot drinks, and wines that can bring out the flavor of your cheesecake and bring a smile to a face.

Manufactured by Amazon.ca
Bolton, ON